America the Beautiful in the Words of Henry Wadsworth LONGFELLOW

Longfellow's writings describe many scenes similar to this highland meadow in Washington's Mt. Rainier National Park.

America the Beautiful in the Words of HENRY WADSWORTH Longfellow

By the Editors of COUNTRY BEAUTIFUL

Editorial Direction: Michael P. Dineen

Edited by Robert L. Polley

Published by Country Beautiful Corporation, Waukesha, Wisconsin

COUNTRY BEAUTIFUL
MAGAZINE

President: Arthur J. Schmid Jr.

Publisher & *Editorial Director:* Michael P. Dineen

Executive Editor: Robert L. Polley

Managing Editor: Charles R. Fowler

Senior Editors: Kenneth L. Schmitz, James H. Robb

Art Assistant: Robert Fehring

Staff: Sharon L. Griswold, Vicki Russi

Country Beautiful Corporation is a wholly owned subsidiary of Flick-Reedy Corporation: President: Frank Flick; Vice President and General Manager: Michael P. Dineen; Treasurer and Secretary: August Caamano.

CONTENTS

INTRODUCTION

It is not surprising that Henry Wadsworth Longfellow is, on the whole, a poet of affirmation rather than rejection. Unlike writers who center their work on conflict and dissatisfaction, Longfellow seems generally to have accepted the time, place and circumstances in which he lived and wrote. In return, the reading public and literary world of his time held the man and his work in high regard. But it would be a mistake to conclude from this that Longfellow's life was one of unbroken serenity and good fortune.

Born in the bustling seaside port of Portland, Maine, Longfellow's sensibility was formed by the presence of the sea. He spent his happy boyhood as a member of one of the town's old respected families. His mother's family was descended from John and Priscilla Alden and Longfellow was early interested in American history. His father, a lawyer and politician, had a small but excellent library of which his son made good use. Longfellow read eighteenth-century authors such as Oliver Goldsmith and William Cowper and older contemporaries such as Sir Walter Scott. His formal schooling, as good as any available at the time, was mainly literary and classical. Although his father was a Harvard man, Henry was sent to Bowdoin College, Brunswick, Maine, where he began his studies at the age of 15. Among his fellow students were future President Franklin Pierce and author Nathaniel Hawthorne.

After graduation Longfellow went to Europe for three years to study foreign languages in preparation for teaching. On his return he became professor of modern languages at Bowdoin and later was appointed to a similar position at Harvard. So, in 1835, he again went to Europe to prepare himself but disaster struck in Rotterdam when his wife, to whom he had been happily married for four years, died.

Months later in Switzerland he met Frances Appleton, daughter of a Boston merchant, and he fell in love with her. For several years she failed to return his affections, but they were finally married in 1843. The greatest tragedy of his life occurred in 1861 when he saw his wife accidentally burn to death when some curling irons became overheated, igniting her hair and clothing. He suffered severe burns in trying to save her and for some time his grief interrupted his creative life.

Longfellow's work became immensely popular early in his career and he was undoubtedly the most beloved American poet of the 19th century. About the turn of the century, however, his reputation among critics began a decline from which it has never fully recovered. Originality and profundity are not outstanding qualities in his work. Literature rather than life was the source of his art.

HENRY WADSWORTH LONGFELLOW (1807-1882)

He was, however, an extremely talented craftsman and, although he wrote in the European tradition, he did much to memorialize American history and folklore. Such poems as "Paul Revere's Ride," "The Courtship of Miles Standish," "The Song of Hiawatha" and "The Wreck of the Hesperus" have become touchstones of American heritage. Even today it is probably true that no American poet is known in as many American homes as Longfellow. This may be based in part on his pervasive presence in American school books, but it is also due to a response to some things which are an inseparable part of the American consciousness. Longfellow's largeness of theme, generosity of spirit, his ability to make direct statements with grace and to sustain long passages of dramatic narrative are qualities which make him a poet forever to be read, enjoyed and genuinely admired.

So when storms of wild emotion
     Strike the ocean
Of the poet's soul, erelong
From each cave and rocky fastness,
     In its vastness,
Floats some fragment of a song.

I

The Sound of the Sea

A voice out of the silence of the de

Longfellow, who often wrote of the sea, lived most of his life within a few miles of the ocean.

sound mysteriously multiplied . . .

FPG by Robert W. Young

THE SOUND OF THE SEA

The sea awoke at midnight from its sleep,
   And round the pebbly beaches far and wide
   I heard the first wave of the rising tide
   Rush onward with uninterrupted sweep;

A voice out of the silence of the deep,
   A sound mysteriously multiplied
   As of a cataract from the mountain's side,
   Or roar of winds upon a wooded steep.

So comes to us at times, from the unknown
   And inaccessible solitudes of being,
   The rushing of the sea-tides of the soul;

And inspirations, that we deem our own,
   Are some divine foreshadowing and foreseeing
   Of things beyond our reason or control.

The New England coast is frequently struck by fierce North Atlantic storms which leave shipwrecks in their paths.

THE WRECK
OF THE HESPERUS

It was the schooner Hesperus,
    That sailed the wintry sea;
And the skipper had taken his little daughtèr,
    To bear him company.

Blue were her eyes as the fairy-flax,
    Her cheeks like the dawn of day,
And her bosom white as the hawthorn buds,
    That ope in the month of May.

The skipper he stood beside the helm,
    His pipe was in his mouth,
And he watched how the veering flaw did blow
    The smoke now West, now South.

Then up and spake an old Sailòr,
    Had sailed to the Spanish Main,
"I pray thee, put into yonder port,
    For I fear a hurricane.

"Last night, the moon had a golden ring,
    And to-night no moon we see!"
The skipper, he blew a whiff from his pipe,
    And a scornful laugh laughed he.

Colder and louder blew the wind,
    A gale from the Northeast,
The snow fell hissing in the brine,
    And the billows frothed like yeast.

At daybreak on the bleak sea-beach . . .

Down came the storm, and smote amain
    The vessel in its strength;
She shuddered and paused, like a frighted steed,
    Then leaped her cable's length.

"Come hither! come hither! my little daughtèr,
    And do not tremble so;
For I can weather the roughest gale
    That ever wind did blow."

He wrapped her warm in his seaman's coat
    Against the stinging blast;
He cut a rope from a broken spar,
    And bound her to the mast.

"O father! I hear the church-bells ring,
    Oh say, What may it be?"
"'Tis a fog-bell on a rock-bound coast!"—
    And he steered for the open sea.

"O father! I hear the sound of guns,
    Oh say, what may it be?"
"Some ship in distress, that cannot live
    In such an angry sea!"

"O father! I see a gleaming light,
    Oh say, what may it be?"
But the father answered never a word,
    A frozen corpse was he.

Lashed to the helm, all stiff and stark,
    With his face turned to the skies,
The lantern gleamed through the gleaming snow
    On his fixed and glassy eyes.

Then the maiden clasped her hands and prayed
    That savèd she might be;
And she thought of Christ, who stilled the wave,
    On the Lake of Galilee.

And fast through the midnight dark and drear,
    Through the whistling sleet and snow,
Like a sheeted ghost, the vessel swept
    Tow'rds the reef of Norman's Woe.

And ever the fitful gusts between
    A sound came from the land;
It was the sound of the trampling surf
    On the rocks and the hard sea-sand.

The breakers were right beneath her bows,
    She drifted a dreary wreck,
And a whooping billow swept the crew
    Like icicles from her deck.

She struck where the white and fleecy waves
    Looked soft as carded wool,
But the cruel rocks, they gored her side
    Like the horns of an angry bull.

Her rattling shrouds, all sheathed in ice,
    With the masts went by the board;
Like a vessel of glass, she stove and sank,
    Ho! ho! the breakers roared!

At daybreak, on the bleak sea-beach,
    A fisherman stood aghast,
To see the form of a maiden fair,
    Lashed close to a drifting mast.

The salt sea was frozen on her breast,
    The salt tears in her eyes;
And he saw her hair, like the brown seaweed,
    On the billows fall and rise.

Such was the wreck of the Hesperus,
    In the midnight and the snow!
Christ save us all from a death like this,
    On the reef of Norman's Woe!

I heard the ocean breathe and its breast expand . . .

THE TIDES

I saw the long line of the vacant shore,
    The sea-weed and the shells upon the sand,
    And the brown rocks left bare on every hand,
    As if the ebbing tide would flow no more.

Then heard I, more distinctly than before,
    The ocean breathe and its great breast expand,
    And hurrying came on the defenceless land
    The insurgent waters with tumultous roar.

All thought and feeling and desire, I said,
    Love, laughter, and the exultant joy of song
    Have ebbed from me forever! Suddenly o'er me

They swept again from their deep ocean bed,
    And in a tumult of delight, and strong
    As youth, and beautiful as youth, upbore me.

THE TIDE RISES, THE TIDE FALLS

The tide rises, the tide falls,
The twilight darkens, the curlew calls;
Along the sea-sands damp and brown
The traveller hastens toward the town,
    And the tide rises, the tide falls.

Darkness settles on roofs and walls,
But the sea, the sea in the darkness calls;
The little waves, with their soft, white hands,
Efface the footprints in the sands,
    And the tide rises, the tide falls.

The morning breaks; the steeds in their stalls
Stamp and neigh, as the hostler calls;
The day returns, but nevermore
Returns the traveller to the shore,
    And the tide rises, the tide falls.

A stretch of beach vacant except for a few pilings and the seagulls overhead.

When descends on the Atlantic

the gigantic storm-wind . . .

SEAWEED

When descends on the Atlantic
  The gigantic
Storm-wind of the equinox,
Landward in his wrath he scourges
  The toiling surges,
Laden with seaweed from the rocks:

From Bermuda's reefs; from edges
  Of sunken ledges,
In some far-off, bright Azore;
From Bahama, and the dashing,
  Silver-flashing
Surges of San Salvadore;

From the tumbling surf, that buries
  The Orkneyan skerries,
Answering the hoarse Hebrides;
And from wrecks of ships, and drifting
  Spars, uplifting
On the desolate, rainy seas; —

Ever drifting, drifting, drifting
  On the shifting
Currents of the restless main;
Till in sheltered coves, and reaches
  Of sandy beaches,
All have found repose again.

So when storms of wild emotion
  Strike the ocean
Of the poet's soul, erelong
From each cave and rocky fastness,
  In its vastness,
Floats some fragment of a song:

From the far-off isles enchanted,
  Heaven has planted
With the golden fruit of Truth;
From the flashing surf, whose vision
  Gleams Elysian
In the tropic clime of Youth;

From the strong Will, and the Endeavor
  That forever
Wrestle with the tides of Fate;
From the wreck of Hopes far-scattered,
  Tempest-shattered,
Floating waste and desolate; —

Ever drifting, drifting, drifting
  On the shifting
Currents of the restless heart;
Till at length in books recorded,
  They, like hoarded
Household words, no more depart.

Leanore Cattani

THE LIGHTHOUSE

The rocky ledge runs far into the sea,
  And on its outer point, some miles away,
The Lighthouse lifts its massive masonry,
  A pillar of fire by night, of cloud by day.

Even at this distance I can see the tides,
  Upheaving, break unheard along its base,
A speechless wrath, that rises and subsides
  In the white lip and tremor of the face.

And as the evening darkens, lo! how bright,
  Through the deep purple of the twilight air,
Beams forth the sudden radiance of its light
  With strange, unearthly splendor in the glare!

Not one alone; from each projecting cape
  And perilous reef along the ocean's verge,
Starts into life a dim, gigantic shape,
  Holding its lantern o'er the restless surge.

Like the great giant Christopher it stands
  Upon the brink of the tempestuous wave,
Wading far out among the rocks and sands,
  The night-o'ertaken mariner to save.

(Continued on next page)

Many old lighthouses still stand
along the New England coast.

Steadfast, serene, immovable, quenchless flame . . .

And the great ships sail outward and return,
  Bending and bowing o'er the billowy swells,
And ever joyful, as they see it burn,
  They wave their silent welcomes and farewells.

They come forth from the darkness, and their sails
  Gleam for a moment only in the blaze,
And eager faces, as the light unveils,
  Gaze at the tower, and vanish while they gaze.

The mariner remembers when a child,
  On his first voyage, he saw it fade and sink;
And when, returning from adventures wild,
  He saw it rise again o'er ocean's brink.

Steadfast, serene, immovable, the same
  Year after year, through all the silent night
Burns on forevermore that quenchless flame,
  Shines on that inextinguishable light!

It sees the ocean to its bosom clasp
  The rocks and sea-sand with the kiss of peace;
It sees the wild winds lift it in their grasp
  And hold it up, and shake it like a fleece.

The startled waves leap over it; the storm
  Smites it with all the scourges of the rain,
And steadily against its solid form
  Press the great shoulders of the hurricane.

The sea-bird wheeling round it, with the din
  Of wings and winds and solitary cries,
Blinded and maddened by the light within,
  Dashes himself against the glare, and dies.

A new Prometheus, chained upon the rock,
  Still grasping in his hand the fire of Jove,
It does not hear the cry, nor heed the shock,
  But hails the mariner with words of love.

"Sail on!" it says, "sail on, ye stately ships!
  And with your floating bridge the ocean span;
Be mine to guard this light from all eclipse,
  Be yours to bring man nearer unto man!"

A SUMMER DAY BY THE SEA

The sun is set; and in his latest beams
    Yon little cloud of ashen gray and gold,
    Slowly upon the amber air unrolled,
    The falling mantle of the Prophet seems.
From the dim headlands many a light-house gleams.
    The street-lamps of the ocean; and behold,
    O'erhead the banners of the night unfold;
    The day hath passed into the land of dreams.
O summer day beside the joyous sea!
    O summer day so wonderful and white,
    So full of gladness and so full of pain!
Forever and forever shalt thou be
    To some the gravestone of a dead delight,
    To some the landmark of a new domain.

Wallace Kirkland

22

wly upon the amber air unrolled . . .

Longfellow described twilight scenes, such as this one, in several poems.

As I gaze upon the sea, all the old

romantic legends come back to me . . .

There is an abundance of romantic legend about Cape Hatteras, North Carolina, the site of many shipwrecks.

THE SECRET OF THE SEA

Ah! what pleasant visions haunt me
  As I gaze upon the sea!
All the old romantic legends,
  All my dreams, come back to me.

Sails of silk and ropes of sandal,
  Such as gleam in ancient lore;
And the singing of the sailors,
  And the answer from the shore!

Most of all, the Spanish ballad
  Haunts me oft, and tarries long,
Of the noble Count Arnaldos
  And the sailor's mystic song.

Like the long waves on a sea-beach,
  Where the sand as silver shines,
With a soft, monotonous cadence,
  Flow its unrhymed lyric lines; —

Telling how the Count Arnaldos,
  With his hawk upon his hand,
Saw a fair and stately galley,
  Steering onward to the land; —

How he heard the ancient helmsman
  Chant a song so wild and clear,
That the sailing sea-bird slowly
  Poised upon the mast to hear,

Till his soul was full of longing,
  And he cried, with impulse strong, —
"Helmsman! for the love of heaven,
  Teach me, too, that wondrous song!"

"Wouldst thou," — so the helmsman answered,
  "Learn the secret of the sea?
Only those who brave its dangers
  Comprehend its mystery!"

In each sail that skims the horizon,
  In each landward-blowing breeze,
I behold that stately galley,
  Hear those mournful melodies;

Till my soul is full of longing
  For the secret of the sea,
And the heart of the great ocean
  Sends a thrilling pulse through me.

Not far away we saw the port, the strange, silent town . . .

THE FIRE OF DRIFTWOOD
Devereux Farm, near Marblehead

We sat within the farm-house old,
  Whose windows, looking o'er the bay,
Gave to the sea-breeze damp and cold
  An easy entrance, night and day.

Not far away we saw the port,
  The strange, old-fashioned, silent town,
The lighthouse, the dismantled fort,
  The wooden houses, quaint and brown.

We sat and talked until the night,
  Descending, filled the little room;
Our faces faded from the sight,
  Our voices only broke the gloom.

We spake of many a vanished scene,
  Of what we once had thought and said,
Of what had been, and might have been,
  And who was changed, and who was dead;

And all that fills the hearts of friends,
  When first they feel, with secret pain,
Their lives thenceforth have separate ends,
  And never can be one again;

The first slight swerving of the heart,
  That words are powerless to express,
And leave it still unsaid in part,
  Or say it in too great excess.

The very tones in which we spake
  Had something strange, I could but mark;
The leaves of memory seemed to make
  A mournful rustling in the dark.

Oft died the words upon our lips,
  As suddenly, from out the fire
Built of the wreck of stranded ships,
  The flames would leap and then expire.

And, as their splendor flashed and failed,
  We thought of wrecks upon the main,
Of ships dismasted, that were hailed
  And sent no answer back again.

The windows, rattling in their frames,
  The ocean, roaring up the beach,
The gusty blast, the bickering flames,
  All mingled vaguely in our speech;

Until they made themselves a part
  Of fancies floating through the brain,
The long-lost ventures of the heart,
  That send no answers back again.

O flames that glowed! O hearts that yearned!
  They were indeed too much akin,
The drift-wood fire without that burned,
  The thoughts that burned and glowed within.

A quiet, old-fashioned port town typical of the Massachusetts shore.

Cows grazing on a farm along the coast of Massachusetts.

There are things of which I may not speak;
There are dreams that cannot die;
There are thoughts that make the strong heart weak,
And bring a pallor into the cheek,
And a mist before the eye.

II

Lost Youth

Freelance Photographers Guild by Pete Turner

FPG by Jack Breed

Longfellow wrote a number of moving poems expressing fond recollections of his boyhood.

MY LOST YOUTH

Often I think of the beautiful town
    That is seated by the sea;
Often in thought go up and down
The pleasant streets of that dear old town,
    And my youth comes back to me.
      And a verse of a Lapland song
      Is haunting my memory still:
      "A boy's will is the wind's will,
And the thoughts of youth are long, long thoughts."

I can see the shadowy lines of its trees,
    And catch, in sudden gleams,
The sheen of the far-surrounding seas,
And islands that were the Hesperides
    Of all my boyish dreams.
      And the burden of that old song,
      It murmurs and whispers still:
      "A boy's will is the wind's will,
And the thoughts of youth are long, long thoughts."

The thoughts of youth are long, long thoughts . . .

I remember the black wharves and the slips,
    And the sea-tides tossing free;
And Spanish sailors with bearded lips,
And the beauty and mystery of the ships,
    And the magic of the sea.
      And the voice of that wayward song
      Is singing and saying still:
      "A boy's will is the wind's will,
And the thoughts of youth are long, long thoughts."

I remember the bulwarks by the shore,
    And the fort upon the hill;
The sunrise gun, with its hollow roar,
The drum-beat repeated o'er and o'er,
    And the bugle wild and shrill.
      And the music of that old song
      Throbs in my memory still:
      "A boy's will is the wind's will,
And the thoughts of youth are long, long thoughts."

I remember the sea-fight far away,
    How it thundered o'er the tide!
And the dead captains, as they lay
In their graves, o'erlooking the tranquil bay
    Where they in battle died.
      And the sound of that mournful song
      Goes through me with a thrill:
      "A boy's will is the wind's will,
And the thoughts of youth are long, long thoughts."

I can see the breezy dome of groves,
    The shadows of Deering's Woods;
And the friendships old and the early loves
Come back with a Sabbath sound, as of doves
    In quiet neighborhoods.
      And the verse of that sweet old song,
      It flutters and murmurs still:
      "A boy's will is the wind's will,
And the thoughts of youth are long, long thoughts."

My heart goes back to wander among days that were . . .

I remember the gleams and glooms that dart
    Across the school-boy's brain;
The song and the silence in the heart,
That in part are prophecies, and in part
    Are longings wild and vain.
        And the voice of that fitful song
        Sings on, and is never still:
        "A boy's will is the wind's will,
And the thoughts of youth are long, long thoughts."

There are things of which I may not speak;
    There are dreams that cannot die;
There are thoughts that make the strong heart weak,
And bring a pallor into the cheek,
    And a mist before the eye.
        And the words of that fatal song
        Come over me like a chill:
        "A boy's will is the wind's will,
And the thoughts of youth are long, long thoughts."

Strange to me now are the forms I meet
    When I visit the dear old town;
But the native air is pure and sweet,
And the trees that o'ershadow each well-known street,
    As they balance up and down,
        Are singing the beautiful song,
        Are sighing and whispering still:
        "A boy's will is the wind's will,
And the thoughts of youth are long, long thoughts."

And Deering's Woods are fresh and fair,
    And with joy that is almost pain
My heart goes back to wander there,
And among the dreams of the days that were,
    I find my lost youth again.
        And the strange and beautiful song,
        The groves are repeating it still:
        "A boy's will is the wind's will,
And the thoughts of youth are long, long thoughts."

From A GLEAM OF SUNSHINE

This is the place. Stand still, my steed,
  Let me review the scene,
And summon from the shadowy Past
  The forms that once have been.

The Past and Present here unite
  Beneath Time's flowing tide,
Like footprints hidden by a brook,
  But seen on either side.

The seacoast of Arcadia National
Park which is not far from
Longfellow's hometown of Camden, Maine.

From PALINGENESIS

I lay upon the headland-height, and listened
To the incessant sobbing of the sea
  In caverns under me,
And watched the waves, that tossed and fled and glistened,
Until the rolling meadows of amethyst
  Melted away in mist.

Then suddenly, as one from sleep, I started;
For round about me all the sunny capes
  Seemed peopled with the shapes
Of those whom I had known in days departed,
Apparelled in the loveliness which gleams
  On faces seen in dreams.

A moment only, and the light and glory
Faded away, and the disconsolate shore
  Stood lonely as before;
And the wild-roses of the promontory
Around me shuddered in the wind, and shed
  Their petals of pale red.

In the America of a few decades ago the blacksmith served an essential function and fascinated the youth.

He looks the whole world in the face . . .

THE VILLAGE BLACKSMITH

Under a spreading chestnut-tree
  The village smithy stands;
The smith, a mighty man is he,
  With large and sinewy hands;
And the muscles of his brawny arms
  Are strong as iron bands.

His hair is crisp, and black, and long,
  His face is like the tan;
His brow is wet with honest sweat,
  He earns whate'er he can,
And looks the whole world in the face,
  For he owes not any man.

Week in, week out, from morn till night,
  You can hear his bellows blow;
You can hear him swing his heavy sledge,
  With measured beat and slow,
Like a sexton ringing the village bell,
  When the evening sun is low.

And children coming home from school
  Look in at the open door;
They love to see the flaming forge,
  And hear the bellows roar,
And catch the burning sparks that fly
  Like chaff from a threshing-floor.

He goes on Sunday to the church,
  And sits among his boys;
He hears the parson pray and preach,
  He hears his daughter's voice,
Singing in the village choir,
  And it-makes his heart rejoice.

It sounds to him like her mother's voice,
  Singing in Paradise!
He needs must think of her once more,
  How in the grave she lies;
And with his hard, rough hand he wipes
  A tear out of his eyes.

Toiling, — rejoicing, — sorrowing,
  Onward through life he goes;
Each morning sees some task begin,
  Each evening sees it close;
Something attempted, something done,
  Has earned a night's repose.

Thanks, thanks to thee, my worthy friend,
  For the lesson thou hast taught!
Thus at the flaming forge of life
  Our fortunes must be wrought;
Thus on its sounding anvil shaped
  Each burning deed and thought.

St. Botolph's Town! Far over leagues of land
   And leagues of sea looks forth its noble tower,
   And far around the chiming bells are heard;
So may that sacred name forever stand
   A landmark, and a symbol of the power,
   That lies concentred in a single word.

III

Of Cambridge, Boston and Newport

A New England church at winter dusk.

Freelance Photographers Guild by

IN THE CHURCHYARD
AT CAMBRIDGE

In the village churchyard she lies,
Dust is in her beautiful eyes,
    No more she breathes, nor feels, nor stirs;
At her feet and at her head
Lies a slave to attend the dead,
    But their dust is white as hers.

Was she a lady of high degree,
So much in love with the vanity
    And foolish pomp of this world of ours?
Or was it Christian charity,
And lowliness and humility,
    The richest and rarest of all dowers?

Who shall tell us? No one speaks;
No color shoots into those cheeks,
    Either of anger or of pride,
At the rude question we have asked;
Nor will the mystery be unmasked
    By those who are sleeping at her side.

Hereafter?—And do you think to look
On the terrible pages of that Book
    To find her failings, faults, and errors?
Ah, you will then have other cares,
In your own shortcomings and despairs,
    In your own secret sins and terrors!

38

Where you shadowy woodlands hide thee,

and thy waters disappear . . .

TO THE RIVER CHARLES

River! that in silence windest
  Through the meadows, bright and free,
Till at length thy rest thou findest
  In the bosom of the sea!

Four long years of mingled feeling,
  Half in rest, and half in strife,
I have seen thy waters stealing
  Onward like the stream of life.

Thou hast taught me, Silent River!
  Many a lesson, deep and long;
Thou hast been a generous giver;
  I can give thee but a song.

Oft in sadness and in illness,
  I have watched thy current glide,
Till the beauty of its stillness
  Overflowed me, like a tide.

And in better hours and brighter,
  When I saw thy waters gleam,
I have felt my heart beat lighter,
  And leap onward with thy stream.

Not for this alone I love thee,
  Nor because thy waves of blue
From celestial seas above thee
  Take their own celestial hue.

Where yon shadowy woodlands hide thee,
  And thy waters disappear,
Friends I love have dwelt beside thee,
  And have made thy margin dear.

More than this;—thy name reminds me
  Of three friends, all true and tried;
And that name, like magic, binds me
  Closer, closer to thy side.

Friends my soul with joy remembers!
  How like quivering flames they start,
When I fan the living embers
  On the hearth-stone of my heart!

'Tis for this, thou Silent River!
  That my spirit leans to thee;
Thou hast been a generous giver,
  Take this idle song from me.

THE BRIDGE

I stood on the bridge at midnight,
  As the clocks were striking the hour,
And the moon rose o'er the city,
  Behind the dark church-tower.

I saw her bright reflection
  In the waters under me,
Like a golden goblet falling
  And sinking into the sea.

And far in the hazy distance
  Of that lovely night in June,
The blaze of the flaming furnace
  Gleamed redder than the moon.

Among the long, black rafters
  The wavering shadows lay,
And the current that came from the ocean
  Seemed to lift and bear them away;

As, sweeping and eddying through them,
  Rose the belated tide,
And, streaming into the moonlight,
  The seaweed floated wide.

And like those waters rushing
  Among the wooden piers,
A flood of thoughts came o'er me
  That filled my eyes with tears.

How often, oh how often,
  In the days that had gone by,
I had stood on that bridge at midnight
  And gazed on wave and sky!

How often, oh how often,
  I had wished that the ebbing tide

Would bear me away on its bosom
  O'er the ocean wild and wide!

For my heart was hot and restless,
  And my life was full of care,
And the burden laid upon me
  Seemed greater than I could bear.

But now it has fallen from me,
  It is buried in the sea;
And only the sorrow of others
  Throws its shadow over me.

Yet whenever I cross the river
  On its bridge with wooden piers,
Like the odor of brine from the ocean
  Comes the thought of other years.

And I think how many thousands
  Of care-encumbered men,
Each bearing his burden of sorrow,
  Have crossed the bridge since then.

I see the long procession
  Still passing to and fro,
The young heart hot and restless,
  And the old subdued and slow!

And forever and forever,
  As long as the river flows,
As long as the heart has passions,
  As long as life has woes;

The moon and its broken reflection
  And its shadows shall appear,
As the symbol of love in heaven,
  And its wavering image here.

A bridge in the Boston Public Garden.

Between the dark and the daylight,

when the night is beginning to lower . . .

THE CHILDREN'S HOUR

Between the dark and the daylight,
　When the night is beginning to lower,
Comes a pause in the day's occupations,
　That is known as the Children's Hour.

I hear in the chamber above me
　The patter of little feet,
The sound of a door that is opened,
　And voices soft and sweet.

From my study I see in the lamplight,
　Descending the broad hall stair,
Grave Alice, and laughing Allegra,
　And Edith with golden hair.

A whisper, and then a silence:
　Yet I know by their merry eyes
They are plotting and planning together
　To take me by surprise.

A sudden rush from the stairway,
　A sudden raid from the hall!
By three doors left unguarded
　They enter my castle wall!

They climb up into my turret
　O'er the arms and back of my chair;
If I try to escape, they surround me;
　They seem to be everywhere.

They almost devour me with kisses,
　Their arms about me entwine,
Till I think of the Bishop of Bingen
　In his Mouse-Tower on the Rhine!

Do you think, O blue-eyed banditti,
　Because you have scaled the wall,
Such an old mustache as I am
　Is not a match for you all!

I have you fast in my fortress,
　And will not let you depart,
But put you down into the dungeon
　In the round-tower of my heart.

And there will I keep you forever,
　Yes, forever and a day,
Till the walls shall crumble to ruin,
　And moulder in dust away!

The time "between the dark and the daylight" was, for Longfellow, the children's hour.

BOSTON

St. Botolph's Town! Hither across the plains
  And fens of Lincolnshire, in garb austere,
  There came a Saxon monk, and founded here
  A Priory, pillaged by marauding Danes,
So that thereof no vestige now remains;
  Only a name, that, spoken loud and clear,
  And echoed in another hemisphere,
  Survives the sculptured walls and painted panes.
St. Botolph's Town! Far over leagues of land
  And leagues of sea looks forth its noble tower,
  And far around the chiming bells are heard;
So may that sacred name forever stand
  A landmark, and a symbol of the power,
  That lies concentred in a single word.

From THE JEWISH CEMETERY AT NEWPORT

How strange it seems! These Hebrews in their graves,
  Close by the street of this fair seaport town,
Silent beside the never-silent waves,
  At rest in all this moving up and down!

The trees are white with dust, that o'er their sleep
  Wave their broad curtains in the southwind's breath,
While underneath these leafy tents they keep
  The long, mysterious Exodus of Death.

And these sepulchral stones, so old and brown,
  That pave with level flags their burial-place,
Seem like the tablets of the Law, thrown down
  And broken by Moses at the mountain's base.

The very names recorded here are strange,
  Of foreign accent, and of different climes;
Alvares and Rivera interchange
  With Abraham and Jacob of old times.

"Blessed be God, for he created Death!"
          The mourners said, "and Death is rest and peace;"
Then added, in the certainty of faith,
          "And giveth Life that nevermore shall cease."

Closed are the portals of their Synagogue,
          No Psalms of David now the silence break,
No Rabbi reads the ancient Decalogue
          In the grand dialect the Prophets spake.

Gone are the living, but the dead remain,
          And not neglected; for a hand unseen,
Scattering its bounty, like a summer rain,
          Still keeps their graves and their remembrance green. . . .

They lived in narrow streets and lanes obscure,
          Ghetto and Judenstrass, in mirk and mire;
Taught in the school of patience to endure
          The life of anguish and the death of fire.

All their lives long, with the unleavened bread
          And bitter herbs of exile and its fears,
The wasting famine of the heart they fed,
          And slaked its thirst with marah of their tears. . . .

Pride and humiliation hand in hand
          Walked with them through the world where'er they went;
Trampled and beaten were they as the sand,
          And yet unshaken as the continent.

For in the background figures vague and vast
          Of patriarchs and of prophets rose sublime,
And all the great traditions of the Past
          They saw reflected in the coming time.

And thus forever with reverted look
          The mystic volume of the world they read,
Spelling it backward, like a Hebrew book,
          Till life became a Legend of the Dead.

But ah! what once has been shall be no more!
          The groaning earth in travail and in pain
Brings forth its races, but does not restore,
          And the dead nations never rise again.

Think of your woods and orchards without birds!
   Of empty nests that cling to boughs and beams
As in an idiot's brain remembered words
   Hang empty 'mid the cobwebs of his dreams!
Will bleat of flocks or bellowing of herds
   Make up for the lost music, when your teams
Drag home the stingy harvest, and no more
The feathered gleaners follow to your door?

IV

Of Birds,
Woods and Hills

Across the Sound the birds of passage sailed . . .

Seagulls scattered . . .

. . . over the skies above the Atlantic.

THE BIRDS OF KILLINGWORTH

It was the season, when through all the land
    The merle and mavis build, and building sing
Those lovely lyrics, written by His hand,
    Whom Saxon Caedmon calls the Blitheheart King;
When on the boughs the purple buds expand,
    The banners of the vanguard of the Spring,
And rivulets, rejoicing, rush and leap,
And wave their fluttering signals from the steep.

The robin and the bluebird, piping loud,
    Filled all the blossoming orchards with their glee;
The sparrows chirped as if they still were proud
    Their race in Holy Writ should mentioned be;
And hungry crows, assembled in a crowd,
    Clamored their piteous prayer incessantly,
Knowing who hears the ravens cry, and said:
"Give us, O Lord, this day, our daily bread!"

Across the Sound the birds of passage sailed,
    Speaking some unknown language strange and sweet
Of tropic isle remote, and passing hailed
    The village with the cheers of all their fleet;
Or quarrelling together, laughed and railed
    Like foreign sailors, landed in the street
Of seaport town, and with outlandish noise
Of oaths and gibberish frightening girls and boys.

Thus came the jocund Spring in Killingworth,
    In fabulous days, some hundred years ago;
And thrifty farmers, as they tilled the earth,
    Heard with alarm the cawing of the crow,
That mingled with the universal mirth,
    Cassandra-like, prognosticating woe;
They shook their heads, and doomed with dreadful words
To swift destruction the whole race of birds.

And a town-meeting was convened straightway
    To set a price upon the guilty heads
Of these marauders, who, in lieu of pay,
    Levied black-mail upon the garden beds
And cornfields, and beheld without dismay
    The awful scarecrow, with his fluttering shreds;
The skeleton that waited at their feast,
Whereby their sinful pleasure was increased.

Then from his house, a temple painted white,
  With fluted columns, and a roof of red,
The Squire came forth, august and splendid sight!
  Slowly descending, with majestic tread,
Three flights of steps, nor looking left nor right,
  Down the long street he walked, as one who said,
"A town that boasts inhabitants like me
Can have no lack of good society!"

The Parson, too, appeared, a man austere,
  The instinct of whose nature was to kill;
The wrath of God he preached from year to year,
  And read, with fervor, Edwards on the Will;
His favorite pastime was to slay the deer
  In Summer on some Adirondac hill;
E'en now, while walking down the rural lane,
He lopped the wayside lilies with his cane.

From the Academy, whose belfry crowned
  The hill of Science with its vane of brass,
Came the Preceptor, gazing idly round,
  Now at the clouds, and now at the green grass,
And all absorbed in reveries profound
  Of fair Almira in the upper class,
Who was, as in a sonnet he had said,
As pure as water, and as good as bread.

And next the Deacon issued from his door,
  In his voluminous neck-cloth, white as snow;
A suit of sable bombazine he wore;
  His form was ponderous, and his step was slow;
There never was so wise a man before;
  He seemed the incarnate "Well, I told you so!"
And to perpetuate his great renown
There was a street named after him in town.

These came together in the new town-hall,
  With sundry farmers from the region round.
The Squire presided, dignified and tall,
  His air impressive and his reasoning sound;
Ill fared it with the birds, both great and small;
  Hardly a friend in all that crowd they found,
But enemies enough, who every one
Charged them with all the crimes beneath the sun.

When they had ended, from his place apart
  Rose the Preceptor, to redress the wrong,
And, trembling like a steed before the start,
  Looked round bewildered on the expectant throng;
Then thought of fair Almira, and took heart
  To speak out what was in him, clear and strong,
Alike regardless of their smile or frown,
And quite determined not to be laughed down.

"Plato, anticipating the Reviewers,
  From his Republic banished without pity
The Poets; in this little town of yours,
  You put to death, by means of a Committee,
The ballad-singers and the Troubadours,
  The street-musicians of the heavenly city,
The birds, who make sweet music for us all
In our dark hours, as David did for Saul.

"The thrush that carols at the dawn of day
  From the green steeples of the piny wood;
The oriole in the elm; the noisy jay,
  Jargoning like a foreigner at his food;
The bluebird balanced on some topmost spray,
  Flooding with melody the neighborhood;
Linnet and meadow-lark, and all the throng
That dwell in nests, and have the gift of song.

"You slay them all! and wherefore? for the gain
  Of a scant handful more or less of wheat,
Or rye, or barley, or some other grain,
  Scratched up at random by industrious feet,
Searching for worm or weevil after rain!
  Or a few cherries, that are not so sweet
As are the songs these uninvited guests
Sing at their feast with comfortable breasts.

"Do you ne'er think what wondrous beings these?
  Do you ne'er think who made them, and who taught
The dialect they speak, where melodies
  Alone are the interpreters of thought?
Whose household words are songs in many keys,
  Sweeter than instrument of man e'er caught!
Whose habitations in the tree-tops even
Are half-way houses on the road to heaven!

Somewhere

the birds sing

evermore...

"Think, every morning when the sun peeps through
  The dim, leaf-latticed windows of the grove,
How jubilant the happy birds renew
  Their old, melodious madrigals of love!
And when you think of this, remember too
  'Tis always morning somewhere, and above
The awakening continents, from shore to shore,
Somewhere the birds are singing evermore.

"Think of your woods and orchards without birds!
  Of empty nests that cling to boughs and beams
As in an idiot's brain remembered words
  Hang empty 'mid the cobwebs of his dreams!
Will bleat of flocks or bellowing of herds
  Make up for the lost music, when your teams
Drag home the stingy harvest, and no more
The feathered gleaners follow to your door?

"What! would you rather see the incessant stir
  Of insects in the windrows of the hay,
And hear the locust and the grasshopper
  Their melancholy hurdy-gurdies play?
Is this more pleasant to you than the whir
  Of meadow-lark, and her sweet roundelay,
Or twitter of little field-fares, as you take
Your nooning in the shade of bush and brake?

"You call them thieves and pillagers; but know,
  They are the winged wardens of your farms,
Who from the cornfields drive the insidious foe,
  And from your harvests keep a hundred harms;
Even the blackest of them all, the crow,
  Renders good service as your man-at-arms,
Crushing the beetle in his coat of mail,
And crying havoc on the slug and snail.

"How can I teach your children gentleness,
  And mercy to the weak, and reverence
For Life, which, in its weakness or excess,
  Is still a gleam of God's omnipotence,
Or Death, which seeming darkness, is no less
  The selfsame light, although averted hence,
When by your laws, your actions, and your speech,
You contradict the very things I teach?"

With this he closed; and through the audience went
    A murmur, like the rustle of dead leaves;
The farmers laughed and nodded, and some bent
    Their yellow heads together like their sheaves;
Men have no faith in fine-spun sentiment
    Who put their trust in bullocks and in beeves.
The birds were doomed; and, as the record shows,
A bounty offered for the heads of crows.

There was another audience out of reach,
    Who had no voice nor vote in making laws,
But in the papers read his little speech,
    And crowned his modest temples with applause;
They made him conscious, each one more than each,
    He still was victor, vanquished in their cause.
Sweetest of all the applause he won from thee,
O fair Almira at the Academy!

And so the dreadful massacre began;
    O'er fields and orchards, and o'er woodland crests,
The ceaseless fusillade of terror ran.
    Dead fell the birds, with blood-stains on their breasts,
Or wounded crept away from sight of man,
    While the young died of famine in their nests;
A slaughter to be told in groans, not words,
The very St. Bartholomew of Birds!

The Summer came, and all the birds were dead;
    The days were like hot coals; the very ground
Was burned to ashes; in the orchards fed
    Myriads of caterpillars, and around
The cultivated fields and garden beds
    Hosts of devouring insects crawled, and found
No foe to check their march, till they had made
The land a desert without leaf or shade.

Devoured by worms, like Herod, was the town,
    Because, like Herod, it had ruthlessly
Slaughtered the Innocents. From the trees spun down
    The canker-worms upon the passers-by,
Upon each woman's bonnet, shawl, and gown,
    Who shook them off with just a little cry;
They were the terror of each favorite walk,
The endless theme of all the village talk.

The farmers grew impatient, but a few
   Confessed their error, and would not complain,
For after all, the best thing one can do
   When it is raining, is to let it rain.
Then they repealed the law, although they knew
   It would not call the dead to life again;
As school-boys, finding their mistake too late,
Draw a wet sponge across the accusing slate.

That year in Killingworth the Autumn came
   Without the light of his majestic look,
The wonder of the falling tongues of flame,
   The illumined pages of his Doom's-Day book.
A few lost leaves blushed crimson with their shame,
   And drowned themselves despairing in the brook,
While the wild wind went moaning everywhere,
Lamenting the dead children of the air!

But the next Spring a stranger sight was seen,
   A sight that never yet by bard was sung,
As great a wonder as it would have been
   If some dumb animal had found a tongue!
A wagon, overarched with evergreen,
   Upon whose boughs were wicker cages hung,
All full of singing birds, came down the street,
Filling the air with music wild and sweet.

From all the country round these birds were brought,
   By order of the town, with anxious quest,
And, loosened from their wicker prisons, sought
   In woods and fields the places they loved best,
Singing loud canticles, which many thought
   Were satires to the authorities addressed,
While others, listening in green lanes, averred
Such lovely music never had been heard!

But blither still and louder carolled they
   Upon the morrow, for they seemed to know
It was the fair Almira's wedding-day,
   And everywhere, around, above, below,
When the Preceptor bore his bride away,
   Their songs burst forth in joyous overflow,
And a new heaven bent over a new earth
Amid the sunny farms of Killingworth.

IT IS NOT ALWAYS MAY

The sun is bright,—the air is clear,
  The darting swallows soar and sing,
And from the stately elms I hear
  The bluebird prophesying Spring.

So blue yon winding river flows,
  It seems an outlet from the sky,
Where, waiting till the west wind blows,
  The freighted clouds at anchor lie.

All things are new;—the buds, the leaves,
  That gild the elm-trees nodding crest,
And even the nest beneath the eaves;—
  There are no birds in last year's nest!

All things rejoice in youth and love,
  The fulness of their first delight!
And learn from the soft heavens above
  The melting tenderness of night.

Maiden, that read'st this simple rhyme,
  Enjoy thy youth, it will not stay;
Enjoy the fragrance of thy prime,
  For oh, it is not always May!

Enjoy the Spring of Love and Youth,
  To some good angel leave the rest;
For Time will teach thee soon the truth,
  There are no birds in last year's nest!

From THE HERONS OF ELMWOOD

Warm and still is the summer night,
  As here by the river's brink I wander;
White overhead are the stars, and white
  The glimmering lamps on the hillside yonder.

Silent are all the sounds of day;
  Nothing I hear but the chirp of crickets,
And the cry of the herons winging their way
  O'er the poet's house in the Elmwood thickets.

Call to him, herons, as slowly you pass
  To your roosts in the haunts of the exiled thrushes,
Sing him the song of the green morass,
  And the tides that water the reeds and rushes.

Meston FPG

The great blue heron
can be found in most regions
of the United States.

No art but Nature traced these lovely lines . . .

Pine trees inspired Longfellow to liken them to cathedral towers.

From MY CATHEDRAL

Like two cathedral towers these stately pines
    Uplift their fretted summits tipped with cones;
    The arch beneath them is not built with stones,
    Not Art but Nature traced these lovely lines,
And carved this graceful arabesque of vines;
    No organ but the wind here sighs and moans. . . .

SUNRISE ON THE HILLS

I stood upon the hills, when heaven's wide arch
Was glorious with the sun's returning march,
And woods were brightened, and soft gales
Went forth to kiss the sun-clad vales.
The clouds were far beneath me; bathed in light,
They gathered midway round the wooded height,
And, in their fading glory, shone
Like hosts in battle overthrown,
As many a pinnacle, with shifting glance,
Through the gray mist thrust up its shattered lance,
And rocking on the cliff was left
The dark pine blasted, bare, and cleft.
The veil of cloud was lifted, and below
Glowed the rich valley, and the river's flow
Was darkened by the forest's shade,
Or glistened in the white cascade;
Where upward, in the mellow blush of day,
The noisy bittern wheeled his spiral way.

I heard the distant waters dash,
I saw the current whirl and flash,
And richly, by the blue lake's silver beach,
The woods were bending with a silent reach.
Then o'er the vale, with gentle swell,
The music of the village bell
Came sweetly to the echo-giving hills;
And the wild horn, whose voice the woodland fills,
Was ringing to the merry shout
That faint and far the glen sent out,
Where, answering to the sudden shot, thin smoke,
Through thick-leaved branches, from the dingle broke.

If thou are worn and hard beset
With sorrows, that thou wouldst forget,
If thou wouldst read a lesson, that will keep
Thy heart from fainting and thy soul from sleep,
Go to the woods and hills! No tears
Dim the sweet look that Nature wears.

Out of the bosom of the Air,
　　Out of the cloud-folds of her garments shaken,
Over the woodlands brown and bare,
　　Over the harvest-fields forsaken,
　　　　Silent, and soft, and slow
　　　　Descends the snow.

V

Of Wind, Rain and Snow

The rain, the beautiful welcome rain . . .

RAIN IN SUMMER

How beautiful is the rain!
After the dust and heat,
In the broad and fiery street,
In the narrow lane,
How beautiful is the rain!

How it clatters along the roofs,
Like the tramp of hoofs!
How it gushes and struggles out
From the throat of the overflowing spout!
Across the window-pane
It pours and pours;
And swift and wide,
With a muddy tide,
Like a river down the gutter roars
The rain, the welcome rain!

The sick man from his chamber looks
At the twisted brooks;
He can feel the cool
Breath of each little pool;
His fevered brain
Grows calm again,
And he breathes a blessing on the rain.

From the neighboring school
Come the boys,
With more than their wonted noise
And commotion;
And down the wet streets
Sail their mimic fleets,
Till the treacherous pool
Ingulfs them in its whirling
And turbulent ocean.

In the country, on every side,
Where far and wide,

Like a leopard's tawny and spotted hide,
Stretches the plain,
To the dry grass and the drier grain
How welcome is the rain!

In the furrowed land
The toilsome and patient oxen stand;
Lifting the yoke-encumbered head,
With their dilated nostrils spread,
They silently inhale
The clover-scented gale,
And the vapors that arise
From the well-watered and smoking soil.
For this rest in the furrow after toil
Their large and lustrous eyes
Seem to thank the Lord,
More than man's spoken word.

Near at hand,
From under the sheltering trees,
The farmer sees
His pastures, and his fields of grain,
As they bend their tops
To the numberless beating drops
Of the incessant rain.
He counts it as no sin
That he sees therein
Only his own thrift and gain.

These, and far more than these,
The Poet sees!
He can behold
Aquarius old
Walking the fenceless fields of air;
And from each ample fold
Of the clouds about him rolled
Scattering everywhere
The showery rain,
As the farmer scatters his grain.

He can behold
Things manifold
That have not yet been wholly told,—
Have not been wholly sung nor said.
For his thought, that never stops,
Follows the water-drops
Down to the graves of the dead,
Down through chasms and gulfs profound,
To the dreary fountain-head
Of lakes and rivers under ground;
And sees them, when the rain is done,
On the bridge of colors seven
Climbing up once more to heaven,
Opposite the setting sun.

Thus the Seer,
With vision clear,
Sees forms appear and disappear,
In the perpetual round of strange,
Mysterious change
From birth to death, from death to birth,
From earth to heaven, from heaven to earth;
Till glimpses more sublime
Of things unseen before,
Unto his wondering eyes reveal
The Universe, as an immeasurable wheel
Turning forevermore
In the rapid and rushing river of Time.

After an autumn rain near Mt. Vernon, New Hampshire.

hind the clouds is the sun still shining . . .

THE RAINY DAY

The day is cold, and dark, and dreary;
It rains, and the wind is never weary;
The vine still clings to the mouldering wall,
But at every gust the dead leaves fall,
  And the day is dark and dreary.

My life is cold, and dark, and dreary;
It rains, and the wind is never weary;
My thoughts still cling to the mouldering Past,
But the hopes of youth fall thick in the blast,
  And the days are dark and dreary.

Be still, sad heart! and cease repining;
Behind the clouds is the sun still shining;
Thy fate is the common fate of all,
Into each life some rain must fall,
  Some days must be dark and dreary.

I block the roads and drift the fields;

my fires light up the hearths and hearts of men . . .

Few areas of the country have winters as snowy as those in New England.

THE POET'S CALENDAR

January

Janus am I; oldest of potentates;
    Forward I look, and backward, and below
I count, as god of avenues and gates,
    The years that through my portals come and go.
I block the roads, and drift the fields with snow;
    I chase the wild-fowl from the frozen fen;
My frosts congeal the rivers in their flow,
    My fires light up the hearths and hearts of men.

February

I am lustration; and the sea is mine!
  I wash the sands and headlands with my tide;
My brow is crowned with branches of the pine;
  Before my chariot-wheels the fishes glide.
By me all things unclean are purified,
  By me the souls of men washed white again;
E'en the unlovely tombs of those who died
  Without a dirge, I cleanse from every stain.

March

I Martius am! Once first, and now the third!
  To lead the Year was my appointed place;
A mortal dispossessed me by a word,
  And set there Janus with the double face.
Hence I make war on all the human race;
  I shake the cities with my hurricanes;
I flood the rivers and their banks efface,
  And drown the farms and hamlets with my rains.

April

I open wide the portals of the Spring
  To welcome the procession of the flowers,
With their gay banners, and the birds that sing
  Their song of songs from their aerial towers.
I soften with my sunshine and my showers
  The heart of earth; with thoughts of love I glide
Into the hearts of men; and with the Hours
  Upon the Bull with wreathèd horns I ride.

May

Hark! The sea-faring wild-fowl loud proclaim
  My coming, and the swarming of the bees.
These are my heralds, and behold! my name
  Is written in blossoms on the hawthorn-trees.
I tell the mariner when to sail the seas;
  I waft o'er all the land from far away
The breath and bloom of the Hesperides,
  My birthplace. I am Maia. I am May.

June

Mine is the Month of Roses; yes, and mine
  The Month of Marriages! All pleasant sights
And scents, the fragrance of the blossoming vine,
  The foliage of the valleys and the heights.
Mine are the longest days, the loveliest nights;
  The mower's scythe makes music to my ear;
I am the mother of all dear delights;
  I am the fairest daughter of the year.

July

My emblem is the Lion, and I breathe
  The breath of Libyan deserts o'er the land;
My sickle as a sabre I unsheathe,
  And bent before me the pale harvests stand.
The lakes and rivers shrink at my command,
  And there is thirst and fever in the air;
The sky is changed to brass, the earth to sand;
  I am the Emperor whose name I bear.

August

The Emperor Octavian, called the August,
  I being his favorite, bestowed his name
Upon me, and I hold it still in trust,
  In memory of him and of his fame.
I am the Virgin, and my vestal flame
  Burns less intensely than the Lion's rage;
Sheaves are my only garlands, and I claim
  The golden Harvests as my heritage.

September

I bear the Scales, where hang in equipoise
    The night and day; and when unto my lips
I put my trumpet, with its stress and noise
    Fly the white clouds like tattered sails of ships;
The tree-tops lash the air with sounding whips;
    Southward the clamorous sea-fowl wing their flight;
The hedges are all red with haws and hips,
    The Hunter's Moon reigns empress of the night.

October

My ornaments are fruits; my garments leaves,
    Woven like cloth of gold, and crimson dyed;
I do not boast the harvesting of sheaves,
    O'er orchards and o'er vineyards I preside.
Though on the frigid Scorpion I ride,
    The dreamy air is full, and overflows
With tender memories of the summer-tide,
    And mingled voices of the doves and crows.

November

The Centaur, Sagittarius, am I,
    Born of Ixion's and the cloud's embrace;
With sounding hoofs across the earth I fly,
    A steed Thessalian with a human face.
Sharp winds the arrows are with which I chase
    The leaves, half dead already with affright;
I shroud myself in gloom; and to the race
    Of mortals bring nor comfort nor delight.

December

Riding upon the Goat, with snow-white hair,
    I come, the last of all. This crown of mine
Is of the holly; in my hand I bear
    The thyrsus, tipped with fragrant cones of pine.
I celebrate the birth of the Divine,
    And the return of the Saturnian reign;—
My songs are carols sung at every shrine,
    Proclaiming "Peace on earth, good will to men."

Brighter than the silks of Samarcand . . .

From THE HANGING OF THE CRANE

After a day of cloud and wind and rain
Sometimes the setting sun breaks out again,
   And, touching all the darksome woods with light,
Smiles on the fields, until they laugh and sing,
Then like a ruby from the horizon's ring
   Drops down into the night.

AUTUMN

Thou comest, Autumn, heralded by the rain,
   With banners, by great gales incessant fanned,
   Brighter than brightest silks of Samarcand,
   And stately oxen harnessed to thy wain!
Thou standest, like imperial Charlemagne,
   Upon thy bridge of gold; thy royal hand
   Outstretched with benedictions o'er the land,
   Blessing the farms through all thy vast domain!
Thy shield is the red harvest moon, suspended
   So long beneath the heaven's o'erhanging eaves;
   Thy steps are by the farmer's prayers attended;
Like flames upon an altar shine the sheaves;
   And, following thee, in thy ovation splendid,
   Thine almoner, the wind, scatters the golden leaves!

easons caught in some of
most colorful moods.

THE WIND OVER THE CHIMNEY

See, the fire is sinking low,
Dusky red the embers glow,
  While above them still I cower,
While a moment more I linger,
Though the clock, with lifted finger,
  Points beyond the midnight hour.

Sings the blackened log a tune
Learned in some forgotten June
  From a school-boy at his play,
When they both were young together
Heart of youth and summer weather
  Making all their holiday.

And the night-wind rising, hark!
How above there in the dark,
  In the midnight and the snow,
Ever wilder, fiercer, grander,
Like the trumpets of Iskander,
  All the noisy chimneys blow!

Every quivering tongue of flame
Seems to murmur some great name,
  Seems to say to me, "Aspire!"
But the night-wind answers, "Hollow
Are the visions that you follow,
  Into darkness sinks your fire!"

Then the flicker of the blaze
Gleams on volumes of old days,
  Written by masters of the art,
Loud through whose majestic pages
Rolls the melody of ages,
  Throb the harp-strings of the heart.

And again the tongues of flame
Start exulting and exclaim:
  "These are prophets, bards, and seers;
In the horoscope of nations,
Like ascendant constellations,
  They control the coming years."

But the night-wind cries: "Despair!
Those who walk with feet of air
  Leave no long-enduring marks;
At God's forges incandescent
Mighty hammers beat incessant,
  These are but the flying sparks.

"Dust are all the hands that wrought;
Books are sepulchres of thought;
  The dead laurels of the dead
Rustle for a moment only,
Like the withered leaves in lonely
  Churchyards at some passing tread."

Suddenly the flame sinks down;
Sink the rumors of renown;
  And alone the night-wind drear
Clamors louder, wilder, vaguer,—
"'Tis the brand of Meleager
  Dying on the hearth-stone here!"

And I answer,—"Though it be,
Why should that discomfort me?
  No endeavor is in vain;
Its reward is in the doing,
And the rapture of pursuing
  Is the prize the vanquished gain."

All the noisy chimneys blow . . .

Freelance Photographers Guild by Jack Breed

In 19th-century America it was not uncommon in northern states for a house to have several chimneys.

The marsh is frozen, the river dead . . .

SNOW-FLAKES

Out of the bosom of the Air,
   Out of the cloud-folds of her garments shaken,
Over the woodlands brown and bare,
   Over the harvest-fields forsaken,
     Silent, and soft, and slow
     Descends the snow.

Even as our cloudy fancies take
   Suddenly shape in some divine expression,
Even as the troubled heart doth make
   In the white countenance confession,
     The troubled sky reveals
     The grief it feels.

This is the poem of the air,
   Slowly in silent syllables recorded;
This is the secret of despair,
   Long in its cloudy bosom hoarded,
     Now whispered and revealed
     To wood and field.

AFTERNOON IN FEBRUARY

The day is ending,
The night is descending;
The marsh is frozen,
The river dead.

Through clouds like ashes
The red sun flashes
On village windows
That glimmer red.

The snow recommences;
The buried fences
Mark no longer
The road o'er the plain;

While through the meadows,
Like fearful shadows,
Slowly passes
A funeral train.

The bell is pealing,
And every feeling
Within me responds
To the dismal knell;

Shadows are trailing,
My heart is bewailing
And tolling within
Like a funeral bell.

The unique qualities of winter—silence and mystery—often are described in Longfellow's work.

Listen, my children, and you shall hear
Of the midnight ride of Paul Revere.
On the eighteenth of April, in Seventy-five;
Hardly a man is now alive
Who remembers that famous day and year.

VI

Listen My Children:
The Histories

Hardly a man is now alive,

who remembers that famous day . . .

From PAUL REVERE'S RIDE

Listen, my children, and you shall hear
Of the midnight ride of Paul Revere.
On the eighteenth of April, in Seventy-five;
Hardly a man is now alive
Who remembers that famous day and year.

He said to his friend, "If the British march
By land or sea from the town to-night,
Hang a lantern aloft in the belfry arch
Of the North Church tower as a signal light, —
One, if by land, and two, if by sea;
And I on the opposite shore will be,
Ready to ride and spread the alarm
Through every Middlesex village and farm,
For the country folk to be up and to arm."

Many Americans, like Longfellow, have been haunted by the nation's Indian past.

From THE SONG OF HIAWATHA

Introduction

Should you ask me, whence these stories?
Whence these legends and traditions,
With the odors of the forest,
With the dew and damp of meadows,
With the curling smoke of wigwams,
With the rushing of great rivers,
With their frequent repetitions,
And their wild reverberations,
As of thunder in the mountains?
   I should answer, I should tell you,
"From the forests and the prairies,
From the great lakes of the Northland,
From the land of the Ojibways,
From the land of the Dacotahs,
From the mountains, moors, and fen-lands
Where the heron, the Shuh-shuh-gah,
Feeds among the reeds and rushes.
I repeat them as I heard them
From the lips of Nawadaha,
The musician, the sweet singer."

Should you ask where Nawadaha
Found these songs so wild and wayward,
Found these legends and traditions,
I should answer, I should tell you,
"In the bird's-nests of the forest,
In the lodges of the beaver,
In the hoof-prints of the bison,
In the eyry of the eagle!

   "All the wild-fowl sang them to him,
In the moorlands and the fen-lands,
In the melancholy marshes;
Chetowaik, the plover, sang them,
Mahng, the loon, the wild-goose, Wawa,
The blue heron, the Shuh-shuh-gah,
And the grouse, the Mushkodasa!"

   If still further you should ask me,
Saying, "Who was Nawadaha?
Tell us of this Nawadaha,"
I should answer your inquiries
Straightway in such words as follow.

(Continued on page 77)

75

The great dignity of the Indian was expressed by Longfellow in "The Song of Hiawatha."

How Hiawatha lived and toiled and suffered . . .

"In the vale of Tawasentha,
In the green and silent valley,
By the pleasant water-courses,
Dwelt the singer Nawadaha.
Round about the Indian village
Spread the meadows and the corn-fields,
And beyond them stood the forest,
Stood the groves of singing pine-trees,
Green in Summer, white in Winter,
Ever sighing, ever singing.

"And the pleasant water-courses,
You could trace them through the valley,
By the rushing in the Spring-time,
By the alders in the Summer,
By the white fog in the Autumn,
By the black line in the Winter;
And beside them dwelt the singer,
In the vale of Tawasentha,
In the green and silent valley.

"There he sang of Hiawatha,
Sang the Song of Hiawatha,
Sang his wondrous birth and being,
How he prayed and how he fasted,
How he lived, and toiled, and suffered,
That the tribes of men might prosper,
That he might advance his people!"

Ye who love the haunts of Nature,
Love the sunshine of the meadow,
Love the shadow of the forest,
Love the wind among the branches,
And the rain-shower and the snow-storm,
And the rushing of great rivers
Through their palisades of pine-trees,
And the thunder in the mountains,
Whose innumerable echoes
Flap like eagles in their eyries;—
Listen to these wild traditions,
To this Song of Hiawatha!

Ye who love a nation's legends,
Love the ballads of a people,
That like voices from afar off
Call to us to pause and listen,
Speak in tones so plain and childlike,
Scarcely can the ear distinguish
Whether they are sung or spoken;—
Listen to this Indian Legend,
To this Song of Hiawatha!

Ye whose hearts are fresh and simple,
Who have faith in God and Nature,
Who believe that in all ages
Every human heart is human,
That in even savage bosoms
There are longings, yearnings, strivings
For the good they comprehend not,
That the feeble hands and helpless,
Groping blindly in the darkness,
Touch God's right hand in that darkness
And are lifted up and strengthened;—
Listen to this simple story,
To this Song of Hiawatha!

Ye, who sometimes, in your rambles
Through the green lanes of the country,
Where the tangled barberry-bushes
Hang their tufts of crimson berries
Over stone walls gray with mosses,
Pause by some neglected graveyard,
For a while to muse, and ponder
On a half-effaced inscription,
Written with little skill of song-craft,
Homely phrases, but each letter
Full of hope and yet of heart-break,
Full of all the tender pathos
Of the Here and the Hereafter;
Stay and read this rude inscription,
Read this Song of Hiawatha!

Pointing westward to the purple clouds of sunset . . .

From *Hiawatha and the Pearl-Feather*

On the shores of Gitche Gumee,
Of the shining Big-Sea-Water,
Stood Nokomis, the old woman,
Pointing with her finger westward,
O'er the water pointing westward,
To the purple clouds of sunset.

Fiercely the red sun descending
Burned his way along the heavens,
Set the sky on fire behind him,
As war-parties, when retreating,
Burn the prairies on their war-trail;
And the moon, the Night-sun, eastward,
Suddenly starting from his ambush,
Followed fast those bloody footprints,
Followed in that fiery war-trail,
With its glare upon his features.

And Nokomis, the old woman,
Pointing with her finger westward,
Spake these words to Hiawatha:
"Yonder dwells the great Pearl-Feather,
Megissogwon, the Magician,
Manito of Wealth and Wampum,
Guarded by his fiery serpents,
Guarded by the black pitch-water.
You can see his fiery serpents,
The Kenabeek, the great serpents,
Coiling, playing in the water;
You can see the black pitch-water
Stretching far away beyond them,
To the purple clouds of sunset!

"He it was who slew my father,
By his wicked wiles and cunning,
When he from the moon descended,
When he came on earth to seek me.
He, the mightiest of Magicians,
Sends the fever from the marshes,
Sends the pestilential vapors,
Sends the poisonous exhalations,
Sends the white fog from the fen-lands,
Sends disease and death among us! . . . "

From *Blessing the Cornfields*

Sing, O Song of Hiawatha,
Of the happy days that followed,
In the land of the Ojibways,
In the pleasant land and peaceful!
Sing the mysteries of Mondamin,
Sing the Blessing of the Cornfields!
    Buried was the bloody hatchet,
Buried was the dreadful war-club,
Buried were all warlike weapons,
And the war-cry was forgotten.
There was peace among the nations;
Unmolested roved the hunters,

Built the birch canoe for sailing,
Caught the fish in lake and river,
Shot the deer and trapped the beaver;
Unmolested worked the women,
Made their sugar from the maple,
Gathered wild rice in the meadows,
Dressed the skins of deer and beaver.
    All around the happy village
Stood the maize-fields, green and shining,
Waved the green plumes of Mondamin,
Waved his soft and sunny tresses,
Filling all the land with plenty.

Wallace Kirkland

Indian life in the past was lived in intimate relationship with nature.

From EVANGELINE

This is the forest primeval. The murmuring pines and the hemlocks,
Bearded with moss, and in garments green, indistinct in the twilight,
Stand like Druids of eld, with voices sad and prophetic,
Stand like harpers hoar, with beards that rest on their bosoms.
Loud from its rocky caverns, the deep-voiced neighboring ocean
Speaks, and in accents disconsolate answers the wail of the forest.

This is the forest primeval; but where are the hearts that beneath it
Leaped like the roe, when he hears in the woodland the voice of the huntsman?
Where is the thatch-roofed village, the home of Acadian farmers,—
Men whose lives glided on like rivers that water the woodlands,
Darkened by shadows of earth, but reflecting an image of heaven?
Waste are those pleasant farms, and the farmers forever departed!
Scattered like dust and leaves, when the mighty blasts of October
Seize them, and whirl them aloft, and sprinkle them far o'er the ocean.
Naught but tradition remains of the beautiful village of Grand-Pré.

Ye who believe in affection that hopes, and endures, and is patient,
Ye who believe in the beauty and strength of woman's devotion,
List to the mournful tradition, still sung by the pines of the forest;
List to a Tale of Love in Acadie, home of the happy.

From THE COURTSHIP OF MILES STANDISH

Lost in the sound of the oars was the last farewell of the Pilgrims.
O strong hearts and true! not one went back in the Mayflower!
No, not one looked back, who had set his hand to this ploughing!
Soon were heard on board the shouts and songs of the sailors
Heaving the windlass round, and hoisting the ponderous anchor.
Then the yards were braced, and all sails set to the west-wind,
Blowing steady and strong; and the Mayflower sailed from the harbor,
Rounded the point of the Gurnet, and leaving far to the southward
Island and cape of sand, and the Field of the First Encounter,
Took the wind on her quarter, and stood for the open Atlantic,
Borne on the send of the sea, and the swelling hearts of the Pilgrims.

Built in the old colonial day,

when men lived in a grander way . . .

From THE WAYSIDE INN

One Autumn night, in Sudbury town,
Across the meadows bare and brown,
The windows of the wayside inn
Gleamed red with fire-light through the leaves
Of woodbine, hanging from the eaves
Their crimson curtains rent and thin.

As ancient is this hostelry
As any in the land may be,
Built in the old Colonial day,
When men lived in a grander way,
With ampler hospitality;
A kind of old Hobgoblin Hall,
Now somewhat fallen to decay,
With weather-stains upon the wall,
And stairways worn, and crazy doors,
And creaking and uneven floors,
And chimneys huge, and tiled and tall.

A region of repose it seems,
A place of slumber and of dreams,
Remote among the wooded hills!
For there no noisy railway speeds,
Its torch-race scattering smoke and gleeds;
But noon and night, the panting teams
Stop under the great oaks, that throw
Tangles of light and shade below,
On roofs and doors and window-sills.
Across the road the barns display
Their lines of stalls, their mows of hay,
Through the wide doors the breezes blow,
The wattled cocks strut to and fro,
And, half effaced by rain and shine,
The Red Horse prances on the sign.
Round this old-fashioned, quaint abode
Deep silence reigned, save when a gust
Went rushing down the country road,
And skeletons of leaves, and dust,
A moment quickened by its breath,
Shuddered and danced their dance of death,
And through the ancient oaks o'erhead
Mysterious voices moaned and fled.

TO THE DRIVING CLOUD

Gloomy and dark art thou, O chief of the mighty Omahas;
Gloomy and dark as the driving cloud, whose name thou hast taken!
Wrapped in thy scarlet blanket, I see thee stalk through the city's
Narrow and populous streets, as once by the margin of rivers
Stalked those birds unknown, that have left us only their footprints.
What, in a few short years, will remain of thy race but the footprints?

How canst thou walk these streets, who has trod the green turf of the prairies?
How canst thou breathe this air, who hast breathed the sweet air of the mountains?
Ah! 'tis in vain that with lordly looks of disdain thou dost challenge
Looks of disdain in return, and question these walls and these pavements,
Claiming the soil for thy hunting-grounds, while down-trodden millions
Starve in the garrets of Europe, and cry from its caverns that they, too,
Have been created heirs of the earth, and claim its division!
Back, then, back to thy woods in the regions west of the Wabash!

There as a monarch thou reignest. In autumn the leaves of the maple
Pave the floors of thy palace-halls with gold, and in summer
Pine-trees waft through its chambers the odorous breath of their branches.
There thou art strong and great, a hero, a tamer of horses!
There thou chasest the stately stag on the banks of the Elkhorn,
Or by the roar of the Running-Water, or where the Omaha
Calls thee, and leaps through the wild ravine like a brave of the Blackfeet!

Hark! what murmurs arise from the heart of those mountainous deserts?
Is it the cry of the Foxes and Crows, or the mighty Behemoth,
Who, unharmed, on his tusks once caught the bolts of the thunder,
And now lurks in his lair to destroy the race of the red man?
Far more fatal to thee and thy race than the Crows and the Foxes,
Far more fatal to thee and thy race than the tread of Behemoth,
Lo! the big thunder-canoe, that steadily breasts the Missouri's
Merciless current! and yonder, afar on the prairies, the camp-fires
Gleam through the night; and the cloud of dust in the gray of the daybreak
Marks not the buffalo's track, nor the Mandan's dexterous horse-race;
It is a caravan, whitening the desert where dwell the Camanches!
Ha! how the breath of these Saxons and Celts, like the blast of the east-wind,
Drifts evermore to the west the scanty smokes of thy wigwams!

As a pale phantom with a lamp
    Ascends some ruin's haunted stair,
So glides the moon along the damp
    Mysterious chambers of the air.

VII

The Hush of Night

Orville Andrews

The darkness falls from the wings of the night,

as a feather from an eagle in his flight . . .

The fall of night in the wilderness has its own special kind of beauty.

THE DAY IS DONE

The day is done, and the darkness
    Falls from the wings of Night,
As a feather is wafted downward
    From an eagle in his flight.

I see the lights of the village
    Gleam through the rain and the mist,
And a feeling of sadness comes o'er me
    That my soul cannot resist:

A feeling of sadness and longing,
    That is not akin to pain,
And resembles sorrow only
    As the mist resembles the rain.

Come, read to me some poem,
    Some simple and heartfelt lay,
That shall soothe this restless feeling,
    And banish the thoughts of day.

Not from the grand old masters,
    Not from the bards sublime,
Whose distant footsteps echo
    Through the corridors of Time.

For, like strains of martial music,
    Their mighty thoughts suggest

Life's endless toil and endeavor;
    And to-night I long for rest.

Read from some humbler poet,
    Whose songs gushed from his heart
As showers from the clouds of summer,
    Or tears from the eyelids start;

Who, through long days of labor,
    And nights devoid of ease,
Still heard in his soul the music
    Of wonderful melodies.

Such songs have power to quiet
    The restless pulse of care,
And come like the benediction
    That follows after prayer.

Then read from the treasured volume
    The poem of thy choice,
And lend to the rhyme of the poet
    The beauty of thy voice.

And the night shall be filled with music,
    And the cares, that infest the day,
Shall fold their tents, like the Arabs,
    And as silently steal away.

The twilight is sad and cloudy . . .

TWILIGHT

The twilight is sad and cloudy
  The wind blows wild and free,
And like the wings of sea-birds
  Flash the white caps of the sea.

But in the fisherman's cottage
  There shines a ruddier light,
And a little face at the window
  Peers out into the night.

Close, close it is pressed to the window,
  As if those childish eyes
Were looking into the darkness
  To see some form arise.

And a woman's waving shadow
  Is passing to and fro,
Now rising to the ceiling,
  Now bowing and bending low.

What tale do the roaring ocean,
  And the night-wind, bleak and wild,
As they beat at the crazy casement,
  Tell to that little child?

And why do the roaring ocean,
  And the night-wind, wild and bleak,
As they beat at the heart of the mother
  Drive the color from her cheek?

Longfellow liked the seashor
during a cloudy and windy

88

Curfew bells were common at one time in New England towns founded by the Puritans.

The curfew bell is beginning to toll;
cover the embers and put out the light . . .

CURFEW

I

Solemnly, mournfully,
  Dealing its dole,
The Curfew Bell
  Is beginning to toll.

Cover the embers,
  And put out the light;
Toil comes with the morning,
  And rest with the night.

Dark grow the windows,
  And quenched is the fire;
Sound fades into silence,—
  All footsteps retire.

No voice in the chambers,
  No sound in the hall!
Sleep and oblivion
  Reign over all!

II

The book is completed,
  And closed, like the day;
And the hand that has written it
  Lays it away.

Dim grow its fancies;
  Forgotten they lie;
Like coals in the ashes,
  They darken and die.

Song sinks into silence,
  The story is told,
The windows are darkened,
  The hearth-stone is cold.

Darker and darker
  The black shadows fall;
Sleep and oblivion
  Reign over all.

Few poets have written more in
praise of night than Longfellow.

THE GALAXY

Torrent of light and river of the air,
   Along whose bed the glimmering stars are seen
   Like gold and silver sands in some ravine
   Where mountain streams have left their channels ba
The Spaniard sees in thee the pathway, where
   His patron saint descended in the sheen
   Of his celestial armor, on serene
   And quiet nights, when all the heavens were fair.
Not this I see, nor yet the ancient fable
   Of Phaeton's wild course, that scorched the skies
   Where'er the hoofs of his hot coursers trod;
But the white drift of worlds o'er chasms of sable,
   The star-dust, that is whirled aloft and flies
   From the invisible chariot-wheels of God.

I felt her presence,

by its spell of might,

stoop o'er me from above . . .

HYMN TO THE NIGHT

I heard the trailing garments of the Night
   Sweep through her marble halls!
I saw her sable skirts all fringed with light
   From the celestial walls!

I felt her presence, by its spell of might,
   Stoop o'er me from above;
The calm, majestic presence of the Night,
   As of the one I love.

I heard the sounds of sorrow and delight,
   The manifold, soft chimes,
That fill the haunted chambers of the Night,
   Like some old poet's rhymes.

From the cool cisterns of the midnight air
   My spirit drank repose;
The fountain of perpetual peace flows there,—
   From those deep cisterns flows.

O holy Night! from thee I learn to bear
   What man has borne before!
Thou layest thy finger on the lips of Care,
   And they complain no more.

Peace! Peace! Orestes-like I breathe this prayer!
   Descend with broad-winged flight,
The welcome, the thrice-prayed for, the most fair,
   The best-beloved Night!

Slowly the landscape fades away . . .

NIGHT

Into the darkness and the hush of night
   Slowly the landscape sinks, and fades away,
   And with it fade the phantoms of the day,
   The ghosts of men and things, that haunt the light.
The crowd, the clamor, the pursuit, the flight,
   The unprofitable splendor and display,
   The agitations, and the cares that prey
   Upon our hearts, all vanish out of sight.
The better life begins; the world no more
   Molests us; all its records we erase
   From the dull commonplace book of our lives.
That like a palimpsest is written o'er
   With trivial incidents of time and place,
   And lo! the ideal, hidden beneath, revives.

From MOONLIGHT

As a pale phantom with a lamp
   Ascends some ruin's haunted stair,
So glides the moon along the damp
   Mysterious chambers of the air.

Now hidden in cloud, and now revealed,
   As if this phantom, full of pain,
Were by the crumbling walls concealed,
   And at the windows seen again.

r Longfellow, night was a time
t made possible new beginnings.

From THE LIGHT OF STARS

The night is come, but not too soon;
  And sinking silently,
All silently, the little moon
  Drops down behind the sky.

There is no light in earth or heaven
  But the cold light of stars;
And the first watch of night is given
  To the red planet Mars.

Part of the constellation known as Taurus the bull, as pictured through a powerful telescope.

The windswept California coastline near Carmel.